12
STEPS OF
ARMOR

ARMOR TO PROTECT &
SUSTAIN RECOVERY

ANGELA PEDIGO

WESTBOW
PRESS®
A DIVISION OF THOMAS NELSON
& ZONDERVAN

WestBow Press books may be ordered through booksellers or by contacting:

WestBow Press
A Division of Thomas Nelson & Zondervan
1663 Liberty Drive
Bloomington, IN 47403
www.westbowpress.com
844-714-3454

ISBN: 978-1-6642-9373-1 (sc)
ISBN: 978-1-6642-9375-5 (hc)
ISBN: 978-1-6642-9374-8 (e)

Library of Congress Control Number: 2023903747

Print information available on the last page.

WestBow Press rev. date: 3/15/2023

ARMOR UP!

12 Steps of Armor is a faith-based recovery program centered around the armor of God as a means of sustaining recovery from addictions, codependence, character defects, and life events that hinder growth. The core of the material is designed around Ephesians (6:10–18 NASB)

> Finally, be strong in the Lord and in the strength of His might.

> Put on the full armor of God, so that you will be able to stand firm against the schemes of the devil.

> For our struggle is not against flesh and blood, but against the rulers, against the powers, against the world forces of this darkness, against the spiritual forces of wickedness in the heavenly places.

> Therefore, take up the full armor of God, so that you will be able to resist on the evil day, and having done everything, to stand firm.

> Stand firm therefore, having belted your waist with truth, and having put on the breastplate of righteousness,

and having strapped on your feet the preparation of the gospel of peace;

In addition to all, taking up the shield of faith with which you will be able to extinguish all the flaming arrows of the evil one.

And take the helmet of salvation and the sword of the Spirit, which is the word of God.

With every prayer and request, pray at all times in the Spirit, and with this in view, be alert with all perseverance and every request for all the saints.

In this program, each step of the twelve-step recovery process correlates with a piece of the armor of God. This program explains how the armor works as it relates to recovery and how we are at risk of our old habits returning if we leave our armor behind.

People learn and retain information differently. This program is designed to be interactive, engaging the participants with visual representations and/or activities that create a deeper level of involvement.

God is growing an army of soldiers, recovery soldiers, and He is doing so using truth and love. People can become clean from substances and destructive habits, but to live soberly is to be sober minded, actively practicing these steps daily while growing a relationship with God and with others. I encourage you to build a team of strong soldiers with activities that bond the team together to build an army for your recovery community.

Welcome to the Recovery Army!

CONTENTS

12 Steps of Armor ix
A Warrior Wears Armor xiii
Where Do I Begin? xvii
How to Get My Armor xix

Step 1 1
    Lesson 1: Truth is I Can't 1
    Lesson 2: Truth Is the Struggle Is Real! 6

Step 2 10
    Lesson 3: The One Who Can 10
    Lesson 4: Who Is God? 13

Step 3 19
    Lesson 5: Turning Your Life over to God 19
    Lesson 6: Turning Your Will over to God 24

Step 4 29
    Lesson 7: Preparing for Peace 29
    Lesson 8: Unpack Your Bags 34

Step 5 41
    Lesson 9: Healing Wounds 41

Step 6 46

    Lesson 10: The Character Battle...................................46

    Lesson 11: React or Respond: That is the Question 51

Step 7 57

    Lesson 12: Pray to Take Away......................................57

Step 8 61

    Lesson 14: Identify Who and What..............................65

Step 9 72

    Lesson 15: Mending Fences 72

Step 10 75

    Lesson 16: Restocking Joy 75

Step 11 78

    Lesson 17: Reporting In..78

Step 12 82

    Lesson 18: Suited for Battle 82

12 STEPS OF ARMOR

1. We admitted that we are powerless over our struggles, hardships, addictions, and dysfunctions and that our lives have become unmanageable.

   > Have mercy upon me, O Lord; for I am weak: O Lord, heal me; for my bones are vexed. (Psalm 6:2 KJV)

2. We came to believe that God, a power greater than ourselves, could restore us to sanity and stability.

   > I will not leave you as orphans: I am coming to you. (John 14:18 NASB)

3. We made a decision to turn our lives and our wills over to the care of God.

   > Let us therefore come boldly unto the throne of grace, that we may obtain mercy, and find grace to help in time of need. (Hebrews 4:16 KJV)

4. We made a searching and fearless moral inventory of ourselves.

   > Search me, God, and know my heart; Put me to the test and know my anxious thoughts; And see if

there is any hurtful way in me, And lead me in the everlasting way. (Psalm 139:23–24 NASB)

5. We admitted to ourselves, to God, and to another human being the exact nature of our wrongs.

   Therefore, confess your sins to one another, and pray for one another so that you may be healed. (James 5:16 NASB)

6. We were entirely ready to have God remove all these defects of character.

   And not only this, but we also celebrate in our tribulations, knowing that tribulation brings about perseverance; and perseverance, proven character; and proven character, hope; and hope does not disappoint, because the love of God has been poured out within our hearts through the Holy Spirit who was given to us. (Romans 5:3–5 NASB)

7. We humbly asked Him to remove our shortcomings.

   For we are His workmanship, created in Christ Jesus for good works, which God prepared beforehand so that we would walk in them. (Ephesians 2:10 NASB)

8. We made a list of all persons we had harmed and became willing to make amends to them all.

   But now you also, rid yourselves of all of them: anger, wrath, malice, slander, and obscene speech from your mouth. Do not lie to one another, since

you stripped off the old self with its evil practices,
and have put on the new self, which is being renewed
to a true knowledge according to the image of the
One who created it. (Colossians 3:8–10 NASB)

9. We made direct amends to such people whenever possible,
    except when to do so would injure them or others.

    So, as those who have been chosen of God, holy and
    beloved, put on a heart of compassion, kindness,
    humility, gentleness, and patience; bearing with one
    another, and forgiving each other, whoever has a
    complaint against anyone; just as the Lord forgave
    you, so must you do also. (Colossians 3:12–13
    NASB)

10. We continued to take personal inventory and when we were
    wrong, we promptly admitted it.

    It was for freedom that Christ set us free; therefore
    keep standing firm and do not be subject again to
    a yoke of slavery. (Galatians 5:1 NASB)

11. We sought, through prayer and meditation, to improve our
    conscious contact with God, praying only for knowledge of His
    will for us and the power to carry that out.

    Evening, and morning, and at noon, will I pray,
    and cry aloud, and he shall hear my voice. (Psalm
    55:17 KJV)

12. Having had a spiritual awakening as the results of these steps,
    we try to carry this message to others and to practice these
    principles in all our affairs.

Whatever you do, do your work heartily, as for the Lord and not for people, knowing that it is from the Lord that you will receive the reward of the inheritance. It is the Lord Christ whom you serve. (Colossians 3:23–24 NASB)

A WARRIOR WEARS ARMOR

INTRODUCTION LESSON 1

> Therefore, take up the full armor of God, so
> that you will be able to resist on the evil day, and
> having done everything, to stand firm.
> —Ephesians 6:13 (NASB)

If you are in active addiction of any kind, you may feel like you are in a battle for your life, your future, or even your next twenty-four hours. You may feel like you are losing the war, feeling exposed, vulnerable, and weary. But when you enter recovery, the active addiction battle ends and the battle for recovery begins. Entering recovery may cause you to feel vulnerable too.

Question: When have you felt vulnerable in your addiction? Describe a time.

Question: How do you feel right now as you begin your recovery battle?

It is easy to feel weary when life seems difficult and stressful or when your struggles are heavy. But becoming weary is a good thing. This may be what it takes to commit to some kind of change, even if it means you feel vulnerable or exposed.

If you have been in recovery for a while, you may be weary, too, for different reasons. You may have begun to compromise meeting attendance, reading, journaling, or whatever practices you have picked up to stay in recovery.

If this is you, now is a great time to begin the twelve steps again, working them openly and honestly to help overcome weariness and the situations that come with it. It can be a dangerous place to find yourself because, up to this point, working a program may be what has kept you alive. But it's hard to self-motivate when you have grown tired of the process or when you have new situations in your life challenging you mentally, physically, emotionally, and spiritually.

Question: Being completely honest with yourself, what are you weary of right now and why?

When you become weary, you risk losing focus and could begin drifting off course. The drift may only feel like it is one degree off course, but that one degree is all it takes to potentially compromise your recovery.

Question: In the past, how has feeling weary thrown you off course of your recovery or some of your practices you do to maintain your recovery? What about right now?

There are many different types of armor. Some people armor themselves through self-care, diet, and exercise. Some people armor themselves through prayer, meditation, and spirituality. But some people armor themselves with fear, doubt, pride, anger, selfishness, and even toxic people. This type of armor keeps people stuck in their destructive habits, making change a challenge.

Today is your introduction to a new kind of armor that is successful and victorious in the battle of recovery and in life. It comes with energy, passion, purpose, and direction. It's called "the armor of God." The Bible tells us this:

> Put on the full armor of God, so that you will be able to stand firm against the schemes of the devil. For our struggle is not against flesh and blood, but against the rulers, against the powers, against the world forces of this darkness, against the spiritual forces of wickedness in the heavenly places. Therefore, take up the full armor of God, so that you will be able to resist on the evil day, and having done everything, to stand firm. Stand firm therefore, having belted your waist with truth, and having put on the breastplate of righteousness, and having strapped on your feet the preparation of the gospel of peace; in addition to all, taking up the shield of faith with which you will be able to extinguish all the flaming arrows of the evil one. And take the helmet of salvation and the sword of the Spirit, which is the word of God. (Ephesians 6:11–17 NASB)

Whether you are new to recovery or you've been in recovery a while, this armor can protect you, fill you back up with joy, and help maintain your recovery. Each piece of the armor of God is an important part of the recovery twelve-step process. As you work this steps study, you begin to put your armor on one piece at a time as it relates to each step.

***Note to facilitator: Next week is a good time to host a meeting night full of praise, worship, and gratitude sharing. This may be done with offering those in the group an opportunity to sing or share inspirational songs, share poems or favorite scriptures that inspire them, and/or share gratitude lists of two or three things with the group. Everyone needs lifting up, and this is a good way to find hope as you journey into this steps program. It's also a way to build a sense of community and friendship with those in the group. At this point in this lesson, you may instruct the group on what to bring for next week, encouraging them to bring their gratitude list if nothing else.

WHERE DO I BEGIN?

INTRODUCTION LESSON 2

A Psalm for Thanksgiving. Shout joyfully
to the Lord, all the earth.
—Psalm 100:1 (NASB)

***Note to facilitator: This is a great time to host a praise and worship night or an outdoor event to find comfort and rest with God. It helps to awaken areas of gratitude in participants' lives.

Welcome, everyone! This lesson is about finding a glimpse of hope for those who are new to the program. It's about getting filled with joy and gratitude for those who have been in a program for a while. It's about inspiration, motivation, and gratitude.

Sometimes life becomes so hard that it may seem impossible to feel grateful for anything. This lesson is a challenge to you regarding a new concept: the "even though" concept. "Even though this is all going on in my life right now, I am still grateful for _____."

I hope you have brought your voices, instruments, songs, poems, words of encouragement, and gratitude lists with you! Let the sharing begin!

Question: Does looking at something you are grateful for help give you hope in other areas of your life? If so, how?

A tip for going forward in this program is to get a journal this week and log three things daily that you are grateful for, specifically about each day.

HOW TO GET MY ARMOR

INTRODUCTION LESSON 3

Come to Me, all who are weary and
burdened, and I will give you rest.
—Matthew 11:28 (NASB)

***Note to facilitator: In this lesson, prepare two concrete blocks that have the words *drugs, alcohol, food, porn, gambling, toxic relationships, shame, guilt, abuse, trauma,* and *pain* painted on each one.

The Lesson

In "Introduction Lesson 1," you read how you may not be wearing the armor you need to win the war over your addictions or other battles you may be facing. You have also read about the armor of God. You may be wondering how the armor of God pertains to recovery. Let's break down the verses that explain what the armor is.

***Note to facilitator: Draw on a board a human figure. Read the verses again in Ephesians 6:11–17, and draw the pieces of armor on the figure as you read them.

Here is how each piece of the armor of God pertains to each of the 12 steps of armor:

1. What is your truth about your current situation (truth belt)? It requires stepping out of denial, which is step 1. What in your life is spiraling out of control? When you can own the truth of your situation, you are embracing the truth.

2. Believing God can help you overcome your addictions and any other barriers hindering your recovery is also embracing the truth. It is the truth about Jesus Christ (truth belt).

3. This step is about surrendering your life and will to Jesus Christ for help (helmet of salvation).

4. Step 4 is about taking your personal inventory, examining right and wrong that has been done to you or by you. This is the beginning of peace for your life (placing one foot in one boot of peace).

5. Sharing your inventory with another person brings more healing. This is a moment when you begin to sever your past from your future, bringing a little more peace in your life (lacing up the boot you just put on in step 4).

6. This next step involves being willing to ask God to remove any character defects that need to change for you to keep growing in your recovery. There is a bit more housekeeping to do. You first need to identify what those defects are for you personally (breastplate of righteousness).

7. In this step, you begin to ask God to remove these defects of character. As you break these habits, you become more effective in doing the next right thing as circumstances arise (breastplate of righteousness).

8. Now it is time to put on your other peace boot. This step involves identifying people in your life with whom you need to make amends.

9. You begin to make amends with those whom you owe it to, as God leads you to do so. Doing so helps you walk with

even more peace in your life (lacing up your other peace boot).

10. Begin taking a daily inventory, and quickly admit when you are wrong. This step is also where you choose to forgive others who may have wronged you during your day. This step is the process of keeping your helmet clean. Carrying unforgiveness or resentment around only causes your heart to become hard, not leaving much room for joy in your life.

11. This step is about remaining in contact with God and growing your relationship with Him. The word of God is your sword. How sharp is yours? The sharper your sword is for battle, the more effective you are as a soldier. The more you know about the promises of the word of God, the more spiritual weapons you have when faced with triggers, hard days, and anything life throws your way.

12. Finally, and above all, take up your faith shield, living out these principles in your life on a day-to-day basis while sharing them with others. If you truly live out these steps and invite God to walk with you, you give God a platform to reveal His strength, love, and help in your life. Doing so grows your shield of faith larger with each experience with God. The bigger your shield grows, the more people you can help as you walk with them. At this point, your faith shield may be growing big enough to shield you both through sponsoring others and being an accountability support for others.

***Facilitator note: Have everyone in the room stand up in a circle or move the meeting outdoors to allow for room. Place the concrete blocks in the center of the circle. Ask for a volunteer to come to the center and hold a block. As the volunteer holds the block, explain to the group how this represents all of the struggles we face when we first enter recovery. When we get to the point in our addictions that we know we need help and begin to share that with others, oftentimes it is our friends in active addiction that we share it with. Ask for a second volunteer to also come to the center. Place both blocks on top of one another, and have the two participants hold them together, one on each side. Not only does our friend want to help us, but they are also often bringing their unhealed traumas and the habits with them. Now both volunteers have doubled the weight and neither is receiving help. They are just not feeling alone.

Now ask the participants who have formed a circle to stand and stretch their arms out as far as they can, side by side, until their fingertips are almost connecting. Ask them, if they allowed God to grow their faith shields to this width, how many people they could fit between them to shield and walk beside them through their journey of recovery as a sponsor. This is an inspiring visual moment for the participants.

By the time you complete this program, my prayer for you is that you will put your pieces of armor on each morning before you ever start your day so that no matter what fiery darts come your way, you will not be harmed.

STEP 1

LESSON 1: TRUTH IS I CAN'T

> Stand firm therefore, having belted your waist with truth.
> —Ephesians 6:14 (NASB)

Step 1: We admitted we are powerless over our struggles, hardships, addictions, and dysfunctions and that our lives have become unmanageable.

The belt in the armor of God is called truth. The Bible explains that Jesus is the truth and the word of God is the truth.

> Jesus said to him, "I am the way, and the truth, and the life; no one comes to the Father except through Me." (John 14:6 NASB)

> Sanctify them in the truth; Your word is truth. (John 17:17 NASB)

Question: What is your truth about where your life is today?

Let's look at what the word of God says about the truth of Jesus Christ.

> The Rock! His work is perfect. For all His ways are just; A God of faithfulness and without injustice, Righteous and just is He. (Deuteronomy 32:4 NASB)

God wants to do a work in you. A perfect work. Perfect does not mean He will make you perfect or expect you to be perfect. He made you. The Bible says that He knows our every weakness. Oftentimes, people think truth equals perfect. They are not the same. Truth is based on what is real, not what is perfect.

Question: How good would it feel to finally own where you really are, if you haven't already done so? What keeps you from it?

Question: Has it become too easy to lie to yourself, and to others, so that you can remain stuck? If so, what holds you there?

Most people expect everyone around them to tell the truth and be honest with them, even if they lie to everybody else. So why can't we tell ourselves our own truth?

> Behold, You desire truth in the innermost being, And in secret You will make wisdom known to me. (Psalm 51:6 NASB)

There is protection in truth. Jesus loves you and wants to help you. He just wants to hear your truth so that he knows where He is invited into your life to help. He waits for you to invite Him in so that He can grow your faith in Him.

> He will cover you with His pinions, And under His wings you may take refuge; His faithfulness is a shield and a wall. (Psalm 91:4 NASB)

Think about this verse for a moment. Pinions are feathers. It feels comforting to see ourselves protected with His feathers while we take refuge under His wings. It feels like a safe place to rest, to feel protected and shielded.

This next verse tells us something very important.

> Buy truth, and do not sell it, Get wisdom, instruction, and understanding. (Proverbs 23:23 NASB)

God wants us to learn about truth: your own truth and the truth of God—not the truth you may have decided He must be because of circumstances in your life. These lies of the enemy, or Satan, have portrayed God to be cruel and unjust in many cases. As long as you believe the lie, you delay healing in your own life, just what the enemy wants.

Once you understand the truth about where your help *really* comes from, His word says to basically hold on to that truth with all you have, gaining wisdom, instruction, and understanding from it. His word and our experiences with Him will show you the truth of Him.

Question: What happens when we neglect the truth, either the truth about God or our own truth?

> Justice is turned back, And righteousness stands far away; For truth has stumbled in the street, And uprightness cannot enter. (Isaiah 59:14 NASB)

***Note to facilitator: This is a great place to have a volunteer demonstrate the walk-away from God. Have the volunteer stand beside you. Explain how we are walking along in our lives and something happens that causes us to pull away from God. So God sits and waits for you, while you take a step away from Him. Have the volunteer take a giant step forward while you remain still. Then explain something else happens to pull you away from God a little farther, with the volunteer taking another step forward. Have the volunteer do this about five times so that they are facing one corner of the room while you are remaining stationary. The volunteer's back should be to you, not turning around. Explain how when we begin to feel the separation from God, we begin to feel the struggle and start questioning God, wondering where God is and why He isn't helping. We do this to the point that we may feel like shaking our fist in the air at God saying, "Why did You let this happen? Where are You?" Explain that God didn't do this. We just stepped away from Him so far that we can't see Him anymore.

Now, have the volunteer turn around and ask God for help. Facilitator immediately runs to the volunteer, slowly walking them back to the path they were on with you in the beginning. Explain to the volunteer, as you take a few pauses on this walk back to the beginning point on the path, how something you are about to experience is going to be tough but that God won't leave them. Do this a few times with warnings, encouragement, and guidance to the volunteer like God does for us. This is a powerful visual experience for the group.

Righteousness means doing the next right thing in each moment we face. If we neglect to own the truth of where we really are in our lives right now, our next right thing stands far away.

> "They bend their tongues like their bows; Lies and not truth prevail in the land; For they proceed from evil to evil, And they do not know Me," declares the Lord. (Jeremiah 9:3 NASB)

Imagine your tongue as a bow that is bent and ready to fire off arrows of lies and denial. It creates more damage and pulls you farther away from the truth: truth being Jesus and the word of God, including all of the promises forfeited in Proverbs 23:23. (Read again from above.)

So what are we to do then?

> These are the things which you shall do: speak the truth to one another; judge with truth and judgement for peace at your gates. (Zechariah 8:16 NASB)

If you want healing and peace in your life, you must first own your truth. If you are new to recovery, you will be looking at this program as a way of battling addiction. If you have completed a program before or are joining the program to overcome some other issue in your life, this is where you need to identify what your personal focus will be for growth and healing. Sometimes people replace one addiction for another. If you find yourself having taken up a new addiction, now may be a good time to work through it!

STEP 1

LESSON 2: TRUTH IS THE STRUGGLE IS REAL!

Stand firm therefore, having belted your waist with truth.
—Ephesians 6:14 (NASB)

Step 1: We admitted we are powerless over our struggles, hardships, addictions, and dysfunctions and that our lives have become unmanageable.

There are many reasons people will not step out of denial. Before we explore those reasons, let's look at what it truly means to be powerless over these things.

Powerlessness often includes holding on to a resentment, unforgiveness, bitterness, fear, worry, anger, etc., and no matter how much you don't *want* to feel that way any longer, you cannot seem to make these emotions go away.

Question: What wounds in your life have you been unable to heal on your own? Maybe you've tried to heal them but either don't know how or where to start.

Powerlessness may consist of lacking self-control to guard your thoughts, words, actions, and choices that you can't seem to stop doing. For example, turning to a drug of choice, anger, violence, self-harm, etc. as forms of coping or handling a situation are some examples of how people lose self-control in the moment.

Question: What areas can you identify at this point in your life that you want to conquer?

The feeling of powerlessness over certain behaviors may still hang around even after you've healed. It may be a habit you formed while having unhealed wounds, traumas, or while in active addiction. For example, are you powerless to control your need for chaos in your life? Have you made it a habit to create chaos in your life to keep from dealing with your own thoughts, kind of like a distraction? Do you look for chaos when living in peace? Is living free of addiction and the pain of old wounds uncomfortable? Chaos can become familiar, being something that you may have lived in for so long that peace is actually uncomfortable at this point. Also, some people choose to live in chaos because they feel it is what they deserve.

Question: What behaviors have you picked up along the way that you want or need to replace with healthy actions?

Question: Have you ever overcome something in the past that you once felt powerless about? If so, what worked for you then?

Question: How have you tried to overcome struggles in the past that did not work? Why did it not work?

Question: Why is it hard to admit the things you feel powerless to control?

Question: Is it difficult for you to ask others for help? Why or why not?

The Bible tells us,

As iron sharpens iron, So one person sharpens another. (Proverbs 27:17 NASB)

> Two are better than one because they have a good
> return for their labor; for if either of them falls, the
> one will lift up his companion. But woe to the one
> who falls when there is not another to lift him up!
> (Ecclesiastes 4:9–10 NASB)

Question: Is it more difficult to ask someone else for help or to ask God for help? Why?

> Come to Me, all who are weary and burdened, and I
> will give you rest. Take My yoke upon you and learn

from Me, for I am gentle and humble in heart, and
YOU WILL FIND REST FOR YOUR SOULS.
For My yoke is comfortable and My burden is light.
(Matthew 11:28–30 NASB)

In placing the belt of truth around your waist, you are choosing to
end the denial. The truth is Jesus has love, grace, and mercy for you.
The word of God holds the answer to struggles, healing for wounds,
and answers on how to trade in the cycle of addiction for positive
change in your life.

If you have answered these questions honestly and fully, you have
just stepped out of your denial, admitted you are powerless over these
things, and have now completed step 1!

> So do not worry about tomorrow; for tomorrow will
> worry about itself. Each day has enough trouble of
> its own. (Matthew 6:34 NASB)

STEP 2

LESSON 3: THE ONE WHO CAN

Stand firm therefore, having belted your waist with truth.
—Ephesians (6:14 NASB)

Step 2: We came to believe that God, a power greater than ourselves, could restore us to sanity and stability.

Last week, we talked about our truth. Now let's talk about *His* truth.

What is the belt of truth in the armor of God? The Bible tells us it is Jesus Christ. He is the truth, and the word of God is truth.

> Therefore Pilate said to Him, "So You are a king?" Jesus answered, "You say correctly that I am a king. For this purpose I have been born, and for this I have come into the world: to testify to the truth. Everyone who is of the truth listens to My voice. (John 18:37 NASB)

Jesus came to prove the word of God is truth. He had been prophesied about for thousands of years, and now He came to fulfill what He was sent to do: to save people from their sins, mistakes, wrongs, and shortcomings and heal their wounds. All anyone has to do is believe.

> For God so loved the world, that He gave his only
> Son, so that everyone who believes in Him will not
> perish, but have eternal life. (John 3:16 NASB)

> For the Son of Man has come to seek and to save
> that which was lost. (Luke 19:10 NASB)

This verse talks about those that are lost in unbelief and sin. His word also says he came to heal the broken hearted.

> The LORD is near to the brokenhearted And saves
> those who are crushed in spirit. (Psalm 34:18 NASB)

Question: What all have you lost at this point?

Question: What has you brokenhearted right now?

Jesus is the truth. We need Him with us every day, which is why He is represented in armor.

> And the Word became flesh, and dwelt among us;
> and we saw His glory, glory as of the only Son
> from the Father, full of grace and truth. (John 1:14
> NASB)

He is full of grace and truth, and He came to save and to heal our wounds. We are called to believe in Him to be saved, but how do we get healing from the brokenness we feel?

And you will know the truth, and the truth will set you free. (John 8:32 NASB)

Jesus equals truth.

If you know Him (truth), He will make you free. How do you get to know him? The same way you get to know anyone else: building a relationship with Him, learning about Him to understand Him.

Have you ever had a relationship grow without putting time and effort into it? Have you ever built a relationship without "showing up" to "hang out?" Many times, people want Jesus to be there for them but never want to be there to get to know Him.

Question: What holds you back from learning about Jesus?

Some people are concerned about what others will think if they build a relationship with Jesus. Others may be concerned with how it may change them or, even more, what it may require of them. They allow these things to influence them until these concerns outweigh the importance of knowing Jesus.

You have a choice. You don't have to allow these things to control you and your relationship with God. Rather, you have the ability to choose quite the opposite.

Think like a soldier. Do you want to retreat, or are you up for the challenge?

STEP 2

LESSON 4: WHO IS GOD?

Stand firm therefore, having belted your waist with truth.
—Ephesians 6:14 (NASB)

Step 2: We came to believe that God, a power greater than ourselves, could restore us to sanity and stability.

For us to be able to *decide* to turn our lives and care over to the will of God in step 3, we first need to know who God is.

Last week, we talked about Jesus, the Son of God. So what do we know about God?

In the beginning God created the heavens and the earth. (Genesis 1:1 NASB)

Oftentimes, people think the only place to find God is in a church building. Church is a great place to find God, along with recovery groups, reading the word of God, devotionals, etc. His word tells us that He is everywhere.

> The God who made the world and everything
> that is in it, since He is Lord of heaven and earth,

> does not dwell in temples made by hands; nor is He served by human hands, as though He needed anything, since He Himself gives to all people life and breath and all things. (Acts 17:24–25 NASB)

> We have seen and testify that the Father has sent the Son to be the Savior of the world. Whoever confesses that Jesus is the Son of God, God remains in him, and he in God. We have come to know and have believed the love which God has for us. God is love, and the one who remains in love remains in God, and God remains in him. (1 John 4:14–16 NASB)

God is love. There is no fear in Him.

> There is no fear in love, but perfect love drives out fear, because fear involves punishment, and the one who fears is not perfected in love. (1 John 4:18 NASB)

God makes all things possible.

> But He said, "The things that are impossible with people are possible with God." (Luke 18:27 NASB)

Question: Describe a time you tried to recover alone or with other people, but without God. Did it work?

Question: Have you tried to find happiness with other people and couldn't? If so, why do you think it did not work?

Luke 18:27 explains why it is so hard for a person to recover without God. It's also why it is difficult to remain recovered if/when they stop going to God. It may be why some people cannot seem to find the right person to share their life with, relying on their own wants and desires rather than asking God to send them who they need.

Question: When was a time you have been close to God and then drifted away from Him? What happened?

Another trait about God is that He won't lie. The apostle Paul tells us in Titus 1:2 that God cannot lie. You may believe God lied when you feel He wasn't there for you in a tragic moment. However, if we are honest with ourselves, any time we felt God wasn't there for us, there were undoubtedly other factors in the situation that were not God's fault. We tend to focus on the part where we blame God for things that God did not do. Our choices or the choices of others are the causes of tragedy.

For example, you may have found yourself in an abusive relationship, blaming God. Did God tell you to be with this person? We can't expect God to protect us when we won't include Him in our choices and decisions. He goes where He gets invited. He will give us wisdom to know how to handle situations in life and decisions we face. All we have to do is ask.

> But if any of you lacks wisdom, let him ask of God,
> who gives to all generously and without reproach,
> and it will be given to him. (James 1:5 NASB)

Wisdom gives us the ability to make the best choice. It is hard for us to know what the best choice is because we don't know everything the future holds or the consequences of the options we have. But

God does. He will guide you along your path when you let Him in to those areas.

Did you get abused as a child and feel like God could have stopped it? Although this is by no means your fault, God gave human beings the ability to have free will, to make choices and decisions. That includes whether they follow good or evil. Both are present in this world. Your abuser chose to follow evil in this case. Satan roams the earth looking for anyone he can get to hurt others.

> Be of sober spirit, be on the alert. Your adversary, the devil, prowls around like a roaring lion, seeking someone to devour. (1 Peter 5:8 NASB)

We are all tempted by the same evil. It's our choice, not God's, whether we act on those evil temptations or not. It's our choice who we follow. God doesn't force anyone to believe in Him or to follow Him. But know this: When someone hurt you as a child, God hurt too. There are many places in the Bible where we can find just how much God hurt by it.

> See that you do not look down on one of these little ones; for I say to you that their angels in heaven continually see the face of My Father who is in heaven. (Matthew 18:9 NASB)

What a thought. To know that when you encountered that abuse as a child, your angel went before the throne of God to see His face and tell of what pain you have endured. You mattered that much to Him that you had your own angel reporting to God what happened to you. This was also a warning to those who may be tempted to harm a child.

Some people are able to heal from the wounds abuse has caused by doing trauma work in therapy or counseling or through twelve-step programs. They may even find empathy for the people who hurt them after much work and healing.

Question: What do you know about the life of your abuser? Have they possibly been hurt in the same way they harmed you?

Question: Have you ever caused hurt to someone because you were angry or hurting?

None of these things were *caused* by God, yet we want to be angry at Him because someone somewhere chose evil over good and we suffered. What Satan doesn't want us to see is that God wasn't behind those attacks. But God is there to heal your wounds, turning them into scars. Scars make great stories and testimonies for others to help them on their journey. No hurt ever has to go wasted unless we choose not to heal it.

To sum up the truth about God, He is with us always. He gives mercy and grace when we seek it. He gives us strength and will never leave us when we include Him. We may go through tough times in our lives because of our choices or the choices of others, but that doesn't change the fact that He will be with us and will see us through. He will heal our wounds, direct our path, and guide our steps when we invite Him in to do so.

> Do not fear, for I am with you; Do not be afraid, for I am your God. I will strengthen you, I will also help you, I will also uphold you with My righteous right hand. (Isaiah 41:10 NASB)

> Know therefore that the LORD your God, He is
> God, the faithful God, who keeps His covenant
> and His faithfulness to a thousand generations for
> those who love Him and keep His commandments.
> (Deuteronomy 7:9 NASB)

Question: Is it hard to believe in God at this point? Why or why not?

Question: What do you believe about God at this point?

STEP 3

LESSON 5: TURNING YOUR LIFE OVER TO GOD

And take THE HELMET OF SALVATION, and the
sword of the Spirit, which is the word of God.
—Ephesians 6:17 (NASB)

Step 3: We made a decision to turn our lives and our wills over to the care of God.

This step is a two-part step: turning our lives *and* turning our wills over to the care of God. In this lesson, we will focus on turning our lives over to the care of God.

Whether you have been exposed to the truths of God in your life or you are new to learning about Him, you may be uncertain about what salvation really is. Don't worry. Many people who have been taken to church all of their lives do not have a clear understanding of salvation.

To understand what the true meaning of salvation is, we need the history and truths of the Bible to reveal the clear picture. Let's start with some history.

In the beginning when God made Adam and Eve, He placed them in the Garden of Eden, where they knew no sin. He told them not to eat the fruit of this one tree, but all of the other trees in the garden they could eat of the fruit. The devil, disguised as a serpent, appears to Eve in the garden and lures her to eat of the fruit of the tree that was forbidden. She then gave some of it to Adam. And immediately they felt guilt. Their innocence and pureness of heart were gone because of sin.

When we sin, we face consequences of sin. One of their consequences was that they were kicked out of the Garden of Eden and made to work and labor hard for food in the heat.

As generations of people grew, sin became more common. God gave the people laws about sin and how to live. When they broke a law and sinned, they were required to bring a certain sacrifice to be sacrificed for forgiveness of their sins.

Time went on, and this practice was being abused by the people and not upheld the way God intended for it to be. So He sent His one and only son, Jesus, to be *the* sacrifice for all of humankind. Jesus was sent to this world to die on a cross as the sacrifice for our sins, and God raised Him from the dead after three days, taking Him to heaven. During His death and those three days, He took our sin and hell for us so that we wouldn't have to. We would have a way to be forgiven since the old system was abused and misused.

Now if you were God and you had sent your Son to be the Savior of the world, wouldn't you want the world to believe in your Son and what He willing did for them? That's the least God could ask of us! And that's exactly what He did.

> They said, "Believe in the Lord Jesus, and you will be saved, you and your household." (Acts 16:31 NASB)

> For God so loved the world, that He gave His only
> Son, so that everyone who believes in Him will not
> perish, but have eternal life. (John 3:16 NASB)

Jesus was a perfect man who committed no sin. He did, however, become sin and took sin to the cross and to hell for us. All we have to do is confess our sins to Him, asking for forgiveness in order to be saved and live in heaven after this life ends.

> That if you confess with your mouth Jesus as Lord,
> and believe in your heart that God raised Him
> from the dead, you will be saved; for with the heart
> a person believes, resulting in righteousness, and
> with the mouth he confesses, resulting in salvation.
> (Romans 10:9–10 NASB)

Salvation is for the sin of unbelief in Jesus. Many people did not want to believe in Him then, and they don't want to believe in Him now. This belief doesn't just come from the mind of a person. It must be a belief in the heart of a person. It's a loving belief and a desire to be a child of God, being adopted into the kingdom of God.

> For God did not send the Son into the world to
> judge the world, but so that the world might be
> saved through Him. The one who believes in Him
> is not judged; the one who does not believe has been
> judged already, because he has not believed in the
> name of the only Son of God. (John 3:17–18 NASB)

Sometimes we feel a conviction or a knocking on the door of our heart, which is when we are being drawn to Jesus. Jesus saves our souls when we call upon Him and believe with our heart.

> Seek the LORD while He may be found; Call upon
> Him while He is near. (Isaiah 55:6 NASB)

Question: Is it hard to believe in the truth about Jesus? Why or why not?

Question: Have you ever experienced that knocking on your heart or felt like Jesus was drawing you to Him? If so, what was the outcome?

His word says Jesus didn't come to judge us but to save us from the consequences of our sin. That begins with believing in Him. He will not just forgive our sin of unbelief, but He will forgive *all* of our sins!

> For all have sinned and fall short of the glory of
> God. (Romans 3:23 NASB)

The need for salvation is not unique to just you, but everyone has sinned. It is a matter of how long we choose to run from it that makes us feel isolated or separated from God and even from others at times. Your prayer to Jesus for forgiveness is, however, personal between you and Jesus. Jesus is the only one who can save you, and only Jesus can give you the certainty that you are saved by His grace. It is a personal experience and a personal prayer. There is no right or wrong way to pray. Just talk to Him with a humble heart and tell Him how you feel, what you believe, and what all you are seeking forgiveness for. It's like apologizing to the dearest, sweetest friend you will ever know!

Question: Does anyone have an experience they would like to share about your salvation, the moment you turned your life over to Him?

You can pray to Jesus anywhere. That's the amazing thing! We don't have to look a certain way, be in a certain place, or have ourselves already "fixed" before we reach out to Him. He is waiting for you!

STEP 3

LESSON 6: TURNING YOUR WILL OVER TO GOD

And take THE HELMET OF SALVATION, and the
sword of the Spirit which is the word of God.
—Ephesians 6:17 (NASB)

Step 3: We made a decision to turn our lives and our wills over to the care of God.

In the last lesson, you learned about turning your life over to the care of God. Now let's look at turning your *will* over to Him.

Turning your will over to God is a moment-to-moment choice. Each moment you encounter throughout your day allows you the opportunity to do what you want or do what God wants. Sometimes both God's will and your will align, but sometimes they don't. Therefore, you have to make a choice: my will or God's will.

> And He was saying to them all, "If anyone wants
> to come after Me, he must deny himself, take up
> his cross daily, and follow Me." (Luke 9:23 NASB)

Notice the word *daily* above. Jesus is sharing that following Him requires denying self. The first step is to deny yourself. What that means is that you must be willing to set aside what you want or expect. Expectations in recovery can cause many setbacks when those expectations are not met. They set the stage for disappointment, especially when those expectations are on others who fail to meet them.

The next step in following Jesus is to take up your cross, meaning to pick up your assignment from God daily and follow Him. You can learn God's will for you through prayer, even if it's in the moment. Asking God for direction and allowing Him to guide you will strengthen you as you go through your day.

> Trust in the Lord with all your heart And do not lean on your own understanding. In all your ways acknowledge Him; And He will make your paths straight. (Proverbs 3:5–6 NASB)

Question: Do you find it hard to trust God's plans for you? Why or why not?

Question: Do you find it hard to hear or recognize what God's will is for you? Explain.

No matter how God speaks to you, seeking His will helps you grow in a relationship with Him. No one wants a one-sided relationship with others. Neither does God. He wants a two-way-communication kind of relationship with you as His soldier so that you don't face attacks from the enemy without guidance.

Question: Who or what would you consider an enemy to your recovery?

Question: Have you ever chosen your plans over God's plans? How did it work out for you?

> Many plans are in a person's heart, But the advice of the LORD will stand. (Proverbs 19:21 NASB)
>
> "For I know the plans that I have for you," declares the LORD, "plans for prosperity and not for disaster, to give you a future and a hope." (Jeremiah 29:11 NASB)

Oftentimes, we are afraid God will require us to give up too much, and we see it as a punishment or as a boring hole in our lives if we do. What we fail to see is the *huge* blessing that we reject when we don't. His word tells us over and over that He has plans for us, and they aren't the plans that harm or hurt us but to give us a future and a hope. It's our own thinking that keeps us from ever reaching this point.

> "For My thoughts are not your thoughts, Nor are your ways My ways," declares the LORD. (Isaiah 55:8 NASB)

Question: Why is it so hard to follow God when it feels like you have to give up something to do so?

Question: Is it any easier to surrender something to God when we, too, want it gone? Why or why not.

Oftentimes, people pray and ask God to just "take it" from them. And they seem to stay stuck and blame God for it. God does not force us to give up anything. That is the beauty of free will. He may, however, ask you to give up something that is hurting you or to remove something that is hindering you from growing closer to Him.

Those things that stand between you and God are the things that keep you from finding peace. But it is so hard to surrender willingly. We would rather ask Him to come snatch it away from us like a child with a toy whose parent has asked repeatedly to bring the toy to them. The child holds on to it tightly until the parent comes and snatches it away. That is *not* surrender or free will. Surrender would be the child willingly bringing the toy *to* the parent when asked without knowing if they would ever get it back. This is an example of the child surrendering to the parent's will, rather than the parent forcing their will on the child.

Sometimes you may not get back what you surrender to God. If it is a hindrance to growing with Him or harmful to you, you may not get back what you gave up. You can, however, rest assured that you will get something even greater! It may not always be something you can hold, but it will certainly be something you can feel!

Question: What is the hardest part for you when it comes to surrendering to God's direction for your life?

Let's look back at Luke 9:23. Jesus tells us this is a daily action. In recovery, we have to focus on twenty-four hours a day. *"Just* for these twenty-four hours, I will surrender my addiction." Walking with God can also be a focus of twenty-four hours at a time. "Just for today, I will follow Your lead, God. Just for today."

> So do not worry about tomorrow; for tomorrow will worry about itself. Each day has enough trouble of its own. (Matthew 6:34 NASB)

STEP 4

LESSON 7: PREPARING FOR PEACE

And having strapped on your feet the
preparation of the gospel of peace.
—Ephesians 6:15 (NASB)

Step 4: We made a searching and fearless inventory of ourselves.

Welcome to step 4! This step is where we roll up our sleeves and dive into the sack of old wounds that keep us bound to addiction and hinder growth in our lives. Some people dread this step, while others look forward to "letting it all out." Some question if they really have to do a moral inventory, and if they do accept the challenge, will it even work?

This step works when you work it fully, meaning you empty all of your hurts out and address them honestly, leaving nothing undone. This step is actually biblical.

> Search me, God, and know my heart; Put me to the test and know my anxious thoughts; And see if there is any hurtful way in me, And lead me in the everlasting way. (Psalm 139:23–24 NASB)

Often people ask, "Why do I have to do this step?" The answer is freedom. Freedom from dragging your past into your present and future. It is also for the freedom to realize you are not what you have done or what has been done to you. Shoving the past down so far that you can't feel it is not freedom. It's actually creating a bondage within you, making you a slave to it. God wants to set you free of it. His word tells us,

> Therefore if anyone is in Christ, this person is a new creation; the old things passed away; behold, new things have come. (2 Corinthians 5:17 NASB)

If you have fully worked steps 1, 2, and 3, God didn't bring you this far *just* to bring you this far. He doesn't just forgive us of our past and stop. Jesus came to heal our hurts. He said,

> Come to Me, all who are weary and burdened, and I will give you rest. (Matthew 11:28 NASB)

So where do you begin? First, you must have a sponsor and accountability team. Some people work their twelve-step programs with a recovery coach, which is great! However, you need to be sure you have a sponsor as well, if your coach is not serving as your sponsor.

A sponsor is someone who commits to support you in hard times when life's struggles or triggers arise. A sponsor is your initial point of contact in those moments. A sponsor is someone who has also completed their twelve-step program and lives out these steps in their lives. They may also guide you through your twelve-step program one on one.

There are some qualities you want to look for in a sponsor, such as dependability and whether their lives reflect the twelve steps on a day-to-day basis. It is important to find a sponsor who will challenge you to push through your hurdles without rushing you through steps you may not be ready for, just to say you completed your step work. It's important for this person to be honest with you and strong enough to point out truth to you in a loving way when they see that you may have fallen back into some denial patterns. It's important that your sponsor be able to share their own struggles and how they were able to overcome them. You and your sponsor should build trust with one another before beginning this step.

Some people find a sponsor and the relationship doesn't work out for one or both. It's OK if the person you have sponsoring you is not a good fit, but do not drag out the relationship to the point you become discouraged and lose hope. Just be honest with your sponsor about how you feel and begin looking for a sponsor who may be a better fit for you.

A sponsor needs to be of the same sex as you. This is very important, not only for your recovery but your sponsor's recovery, too. The reason is because many people in recovery are also battling codependence. Having a sponsor of the opposite sex may create a "need to rescue" situation, leading to an unhealthy relationship or standards to be compromised and therefore jeopardizing both of your recoveries.

Question: When choosing your sponsor, what concerns do you have?

Question: What are you looking for in a sponsor?

An accountability team consists of people around you who encourage you and motivate you to stay on your recovery journey. In a moment of struggle, if your sponsor isn't available, you should reach out to someone on your accountability team for wisdom, guidance, and a listening ear.

Whether it's a recovery coach, a sponsor, or an accountability partner/team you are looking for, it is good to pray and ask God to direct you in your search. God will align you with the people you need in your path to healing.

If you are like some people who think, *I'll work my steps on my own,* you will lack the support you need to fully heal. You will also miss out on a guide being able to challenge any denial you may still be holding on to during your inventory. God's word tells us,

> Two are better than one because they have a good return for their labor. For if either of them falls, the one will lift up his companion. But woe to the one who falls when there is not another to lift him up! (Ecclesiastes 4:9–10 NASB)

As iron sharpens iron, So one person sharpens another. (Proverbs 27:17 NASB)

This second verse tells us we must sharpen one another, not cause one another to become dull. This is why it is important to make sure the person you ask to sponsor you and the people you select as part of your accountability team will actually sharpen you, even when you know it may hurt to hear the truth. This sharpening shouldn't feel degrading but should be done with love for your well-being. Jesus spoke hard truths to the people as he journeyed throughout the land preaching and teaching. It was often hard for them to hear, but it was necessary for growth. Your sponsor should be able to speak truthfully to you in love rather than judgment.

As a result, we are no longer to be children, tossed here and there by waves and carried about by every wind of doctrine, by the trickery of people, by craftiness in deceitful scheming; but speaking the truth in love, we are to grow up in all aspects into Him who is the head, that is, Christ. (Ephesians 4:14–15 NASB)

Question: Is it hard for you to accept the truth, even if you know you need to hear it? Why or why not?

Question: What concerns you about moving forward with this step?

Question: What do you hope to get out of this step?

Question: How willing are you to explore your life to identify pain, resentments, hurt, anger, etc.? Why or why not?

STEP 4

LESSON 8: UNPACK YOUR BAGS

And having strapped on your feet the
preparation of the gospel of peace.
—Ephesians 6:15 (NASB)

Step 4: We made a searching and fearless inventory of ourselves.

In this step, we begin unpacking our bags of all of the hurts that have happened to us and all of the hurts that we have caused to others. Before beginning the inventory, let's discuss what each section of the inventory covers. Below you will find a guide for your inventory over the hurts you've experienced throughout your life. These columns are all necessary in order to fully complete this step. You may write your inventory in these columns in your workbook; however, you will most likely want to transfer these columns to a notebook where you have plenty of room to fully inventory each situation.

12 Steps of Armor Personal Inventory			
Who was involved	**What happened**	**How it impacted your past and present**	**Owning your part**

Column 1: The *who*. This column is where you list who was or is the object of your resentment, hurt, pain, anger, trauma, jealousy, bitterness, rage, unforgiveness, envy, etc. Go back as far as you can remember and be sure to cover all of the people associated with incidents that make you feel some type of way. When in doubt as to whether or not the person or incident is still impacting you, listing it may be a good idea just to be sure you leave nothing undone. Anything that has been shoved down and unresolved will come to the surface as you proceed through the inventory, if the incident still has some type of hold on you.

Remember whatever you leave undone in this step, you will still have to carry around with you in your future until you finally inventory it.

Column 2: The *what*. This column is where you list what happened, what the person did, to cause you the pain and frustration you are now dealing with in your life. This may be the first time you have ever acknowledged these things openly and honestly with yourself. You may have been holding these events inside for so long that you may feel a sense of relief as you write about them. Even though it's on paper, there is great relief in purging these things externally from the places they have lived in your heart and mind for so long.

Column 3: The *how*. This is the point that you own how the *who* and the *what* effected your life in your past. It is also at this point that you share how the event currently affects your present. Whether you are carrying around bitterness, anxiety, depression, questions of why, lack of trust with others, or other side effects of this wound, it is important to fully acknowledge the impact.

This is a self-examination moment. To be self-aware means to clearly see how something is impacting your life and how you have coped with it as a result. This is a time to be honest with yourself and step out of denial about the effect the wound has been in your life. This process can be painful. Keep in mind that finally owning these things allows you to have a moment to grieve over what you feel like you have lost as a result of it.

Column 4: *Owning your part*. Many times, people are so hurt by what the person did to them that they fail to take an honest look at what their part may have been in the incident. Taking an honest look at ourselves in this effort causes us to accept our part of the blame, should there be any to accept.

You do not always have a part in the incident. It is in this moment that healing begins when you realize you honestly had no part over situations you may have been blaming yourself about for a long time. Oftentimes, when something has happened to you as a child, you find yourself accepting responsibility or blame that wasn't or isn't yours to accept.

Question: What concerns do you have as you become acquainted with the inventory?

As you begin your journey, know that at times this inventory may feel heavy, but you are not alone! Reach out to your sponsor, coach, or accountability team as often as you need to so that you don't feel alone.

You will see at the end of this lesson that there are several Bible verses for encouragement as you journey through the past. Before you begin your inventory work each time, pray for the Holy Spirit to help you with strength and comfort. Let God guide you, praying that He reveals to you all of the things He knows are holding you back from healing. Undoubtedly, He can see more than we can, and He is eager to set you free of all of it! It is recommended that you begin and end with prayer and a verse each time to lift you back up and bring comfort to you.

**Facilitator note: This is a good time to share John 4:1–30, reflecting valuable points.

1. Jesus did not care who she was. He displayed that she was worth it when He spoke to her and it was forbidden, being a Samaritan. It doesn't matter who we are. Jesus came to save all of us.
2. Jesus instructed her to get her husband. She shared her truth, that she had no husband. And Jesus commended her by telling her that

she had correctly said the truth. He did not tell her how sorry she was or condemn her for her decisions in life. He wasn't there to judge her but to offer her help—living water.

3.   She then left her pots and went into the city to tell the men to come see him. She described Jesus in verse 29. "Come, see a man who told me all the things that I have done." It was like a moment of doing inventory with Jesus. Notice how gentle He was with her throughout the whole conversation!

4.   This woman didn't have to meet a certain condition to be used by Jesus to spread the news of Him. And neither do you! They formed a relationship there with two-way communication, truth, and love. Jesus loves you just the same!

SCRIPTURES OF ENCOURAGEMENT

The LORD is near to the brokenhearted And saves those who are crushed in spirit. (Psalm 34:18 NASB)

From my distress I called upon the LORD; The LORD answered me and put me in an open space. (Psalm 118:5 NASB)

He heals the brokenhearted And binds up their wounds. (Psalm 147:3 NASB)

Do not fear, for I am with you; Do not be afraid, for I am your God. I will strengthen you, I will also help you, I will also uphold you with My righteous right hand. (Isaiah 41:10 NASB)

Blessed are those who mourn, for they will be comforted. (Matthew 5:4 NASB)

Come to Me, all who are weary and burdened, and I will give you rest. (Matthew 11:28 NASB)

These things I have spoken to you so that in Me you may have peace. In the world you have tribulation, but take courage; I have overcome the world. (John 16:33 NASB)

It was for freedom that Christ set us free; therefore keep standing firm and do not be subject again to a yoke of slavery. (Galatians 5:1 NASB)

I can do all things through Him who strengthens me. (Philippians 4:13 NASB)

For God has not given us a spirit of timidity, but of power and love and discipline. (2 Timothy 1:7 NASB)

STEP 5

LESSON 9: HEALING WOUNDS

> And having strapped on your feet the
> preparation of the gospel of peace.
> —Ephesians 6:15 (NASB)

Step 5: We admitted to ourselves, to God, and to another human being the exact nature of our wrongs.

In step 4, you put your foot into one of your peace boots as part of the armor of God. Now it's time to lace that boot up. It has undoubtedly been difficult to have any peace in your life with these wounds unhealed.

You may be wondering why this step requires you to share your inventory with another person. We share our inventory with God for forgiveness, help, guidance, comfort, etc. We share with another human being for healing.

> Therefore, confess your sins to one another, and
> pray for one another so that you may be healed.
> A prayer of a righteous person, when it is brought
> about, can accomplish much. (James 5:16 NASB)

Sharing with another person creates the beginning of healing. And praying together expedites that healing. As stated before, you should have a relationship of trust built with your sponsor at this point in order to share your inventory comfortably. Your sponsor may, as you share, point out some things you may be overlooking amid the pain of the situation. He or she may ask you questions about your responsibility to be sure you aren't still in any type of denial about your part. Your sponsor may also help you see that you can stop blaming yourself for those situations that were not your fault such as in childhood abuse situations. None of this should reflect judgment. The discussion should be constructive to your healing and done in love.

As iron sharpens iron, So one person sharpens another. (Proverbs 27:17 NASB)

Question: What are your concerns about sharing your inventory?

Question: Have you fully completed your inventory with all of the events of your past that have caused pain, trauma, or led to addiction? Why or why not?

Question: Do you feel you have been honest with yourself in your inventory? Why or why not?

If your inventory reflects that you have no part of the responsibility in any of the events listed, you may want to pray for God to reveal those things to you that you may have a hard time seeing. This is a time to be sure there is no denial lingering for you. It could stall your healing.

> Search me, God, and know my heart; Put me to the test and know my anxious thoughts; and see if there is any hurtful way in me, And lead me in the everlasting way. (Psalm 139:23–24 NASB)

All of us have areas of responsibility that are undoubtedly our fault. The Bible tells us that no one is exempt from mistakes.

For all have sinned and fall short of the glory of God. (Romans 3:23 NASB)

Notice the word *all* above. We have all fallen short of doing the right thing at some point in our lives. Do not feel alone! We've all been there. Hurt people tend to bleed their hurt onto other people, whether it's in revenge to the person who hurt them or involves hurting someone else the way they were hurt.

Most of the people on your inventory have hurt you because someone somewhere in their lives has hurt them. This does not excuse what they may have done to you by any means. It helps to recognize that. Just like we have hurt others out of our hurt, we have also been on the receiving end of someone else's hurt.

Once you have fully completed your inventory and are ready to share, you and your sponsor should set aside a time to share your inventory. It is important to set a time when both of you will not feel rushed. You need time to talk through it. It may take more than one visit. There is no rush, so please do not skim over your inventory just for the sake of getting through it. As with any of the previous steps, if you don't fully work the step, you won't fully heal.

Question: What are some steps you can take to make sharing your inventory with your sponsor or coach easier for you?

Praying before you begin to share your inventory is very important. You will benefit from the help and comfort the Jesus has to offer. While sharing, if you need to take a break, please do so. Deep breathing exercises will help oxygen flow into your body and help relieve any anxiety that may arise and/or calm any anger you may feel.

Keep the Bible verses from lesson 8 with you through this step. It may help to revisit these verses to remind you of your loving caring Heavenly Father, who is working on your behalf and walking beside you through your recovery. He wants to set you free of any shame and guilt of your past. You are encouraged to pray for comfort as soon as you finish sharing each time, whether you pray alone or with your sponsor. It is important to end each time uplifted!

> The thief comes only to steal and kill and destroy; I came that they may have life, and have it abundantly. (John 10:10 NASB)

There is no reason to leave yourself open to the mind games of the enemy, Satan. Praying to God for comfort as you finish each time keeps you in contact with your Heavenly Father, the one working to heal you!

**Note to facilitator: This is a good time to share John 5:1–9. This man shared with another (Jesus, who was just another person in his eyes, not knowing who he was sharing with). He shared how he was hurting physically and emotionally. He felt defeated because he was always getting left behind, never getting to where he needed to be in order to be healed. The others there were always beating him to the water, which indicates that they were hurting physically, too. So their physical hurt and desire for healing left this man to fend for himself. Their hurt (physically) hurt him. He poured his heart out to Jesus and received healing. This healing, however, came from an encounter with Jesus!

Luke 5:17–26 is another scripture to share that reflects the efforts of different friends. These friends knew the way to healing and went to great lengths to carry him to it and through it to get him in front of Jesus. When he is lowered in front of Jesus, he is forgiven first. Then healed.

Both of these stories took an encounter with Jesus for healing. One for physical healing and the other for forgiveness of sin and healing.

Question: In John 5:1–9, once the man at the pool was healed, do you think he forgave the others he may have held some resentment toward for always beating him to the waters? Why or why not? Would you?

Question: Do you always forgive after you have experienced a blessing of healing? Why or why not?

Let the inventory sharing begin!

STEP 6

LESSON 10: THE CHARACTER BATTLE

Stand firm therefore, having belted your waist with truth,
and having put on the breastplate of righteousness.
—Ephesians 6:14 (NASB)

Step 6: We were entirely ready to have God remove all these defects
of character.

Now that you have shared your inventory with your sponsor or
coach, it is time to further train for battle in this recovery army. Step
6 is centered around the breastplate of righteousness.

To understand this piece of armor, we need to understand the
meaning of the word *righteousness*. Righteousness is simply choosing
to do the next right thing.

Some people get discouraged when their thoughts race too far ahead
into the future. For example, thinking that you must be perfect and
live perfectly to remain in recovery is a concept that causes some
people not to even want to try living sober or living for God. They
already feel defeated, thinking they can never be what God expects
them to be. It is unhealthy to place these expectations on ourselves

or others. We must strive to do the next right thing *one* day at a time, *one* thing at a time, and renew that thought each day.

The Bible teaches us the following:

> Finally, brothers and sisters, whatever is true, whatever is honorable, whatever is right, whatever is pure, whatever is lovely, whatever is commendable, if there is any excellence and if anything worthy of praise, think about these things. As for the things you have learned and received and heard and seen in me, practice these things, and the God of peace will be with you. (Philippians 4:8–9 NASB)

In recovery, we seek peace from racing thoughts. This verse tells us what to think about and to "practice these things." You may have heard the saying "Practice makes perfect." Practicing these things one day at a time, one thing at a time, until they become our new habit is how we achieve peace. We begin to respond, rather than react, to life's challenges.

Practice is the same as training, and in recovery and in our walk with God. So what happens if we make mistakes while practicing or training? The Bible tells us,

> But He gives a greater grace. Therefore it says, "GOD IS OPPOSED TO THE PROUD, BUT GIVES GRACE TO THE HUMBLE." (James 4:6 NASB)

Reacting, rather than responding, often creates more damage to work through later. This verse in James reminds us that He gives a greater grace. Pride is one thing God hates, but He sure loves humility. Humility is what it takes to put away the pride, telling God our error and seeking His forgiveness. We need to learn from it and turn from it, striving to be better today than we were yesterday.

Let's look at the different types of character defects. Some examples of character defects are listed below.

anger	anxiety	jealousy	condemnation
lying	egotism	envy	pride
selfishness	yelling	fighting	cursing
laziness	impatience	hatred	vanity
insulting	greed	swearing	blaming others

You may have different aspects of your character that are not listed here that you would like to ask God to remove.

Question: What defects can you identify within your character at this point?

Question: Recall a time you recently reacted to a situation in a way that left you feeling guilty. What happened?

Character defects come from many sources. Maybe you picked up the habit from a friend or family member. Or maybe your habit developed from a learned behavior you witnessed as a child. For example, if you had a parent who always resorted to anger as a means of solving a problem, you may be conditioned to do the same. Your habit may have developed in response to something painful that happened, leading you to develop a character defect as a coping mechanism. No matter where the habit came from, you need to recognize them before you can be fully ready to let God remove them.

Question: Do you want your character defects removed? Why or why not?

Question: What is the most difficult part about letting go of your character defects?

Some people don't want to let go of their character defects because they don't know who they will be without them. For example, some people take pride in fighting or in their anger. They may be afraid if they surrender their anger, they will become weak. This is not true. The Bible contains numerous verses about the word *meek*. If you search out these verses, you will see that being meek (which society oftentimes sees as being weak) takes much more effort and strength than being angry. It is a good idea to read these verses to gain an understanding of God's view of what true strength looks like.

Our character defects have been our suits of armor for a long time. And that armor has failed us, undoubtedly, many times. Our new armor, the armor of God, causes us to act in the fruits of the Spirit, not *our* character defects.

> But the fruit of the Spirit is love, joy, peace, patience, kindness, goodness, faithfulness, gentleness, self-control; against such things there is no law. Now those who belong to Christ Jesus have crucified the flesh with its passions and desires. If we live by the Spirit, let's follow the Spirit as well. Let's not become boastful, challenging one another, envying one another. (Galatians 5:22–26 NASB)

Question: Why should you trade in your character defects in for the armor of God?

Question: What do you think surrendering your character defects will do for you personally?

STEP 6

LESSON 11: REACT OR RESPOND: THAT IS THE QUESTION

Stand firm therefore, having belted your waist with truth,
and having put on the breastplate of righteousness.
—Ephesians 6:14 (NASB)

Step 6: We were entirely ready to have God remove all these defects of character.

In the last lesson, we explored different character defects and some of the reasons we react the way we do. We also saw how reacting negatively causes wounds for ourselves and for others. Reacting to situations oftentimes creates guilt, shame, and other habits we have fought so hard to break.

Think of responding as a positive charge and reacting as a negative charge. Responding builds up. Reacting tears down. Making a choice to respond helps maintain sanity. Sanity is being willing to change or do something different that is self-controlled and promotes a sound mind.

> Now for this very reason also, applying all diligence, in your faith supply moral excellence, and in your moral excellence, knowledge, and in your knowledge, self-control, and in your self-control, perseverance, and in your perseverance, godliness, and in your godliness, brotherly kindness, and in your brotherly kindness, love. For if these qualities are yours and are increasing, they do not make you useless nor unproductive in the true knowledge of our Lord Jesus Christ. (2 Peter 1:5–8 NASB)

We trade in the old for the new in order to thrive in our recovery, our lives, and our walk with God.

Question: Have you ever caught yourself about to react to a situation, paused a moment, and chosen a different response? Share an example and the outcome.

Let's look at some ways our character defects have become our negative reactions. We do this through character inventory. Character inventory involves looking back at recent situations we've experienced that led to a character defect reaction. This inventory is different from the personal moral inventory in step 4. Moral inventory required you to go back as far as you could remember and list all of your hurts, resentments, and people you have hurt.

Character inventory centers around the most recent situations you have experienced, preferably the most recent five to ten instances. It focuses on the situations that caused you to react in a negative way. Let's look at the columns in this inventory for a better understanding.

12 Steps of Armor Character Inventory			
The Situation	**The Temptation Method**	**My Reaction**	**Possible Response**
	1. Lust of the flesh— something we want to satisfy a physical or emotional need. _____ 2. Lust of the eyes— something we want to own or possess. _____ 3. Pride of life attacks our ego or causes us to think more highly of ourselves.		**Fruits of the Spirit** Love, Joy, Peace Patience, Kindness Goodness, Gentleness, Faithfulness, Self-Control

Column 1: The Situation

In this column, list some of the most recent situations that left you feeling frustrated, angry, or some type of negative way.

Column 2: The Temptation Method

Many things we encounter in life may make us feel angry, frustrated, or some other negative emotion. Feeling these emotions is not always wrong. The wrong often comes from what happens next. Did you act on that feeling or emotion? If so, was it a negative reaction or a positive response?

The Bible explains how we become tempted to react in situations we encounter. We generally get provoked by three temptations. These are listed above in column 2 with a description of each one. The Bible tells us that these things are not of God.

> For all that is in the world, the lust of the flesh and the lust of the eyes and the boastful pride of life, is not from the Father, but is from the world. (1 John 2:16 NASB)

**Facilitator note: Review the three temptations above.

Even Jesus, when He was here on earth, was tempted by these same temptations. Reading Matthew 4:1–11, you can see how He was tempted and what He did to resist it.

**Facilitator note: Read this scripture with the group or individual, pointing out the temptation type as you explore the scripture. You may also relate this experience to Eve in the Garden of Eden when she was tempted by the serpent to eat of the fruit of the forbidden tree.

In this inventory, you should now be able to identify how you were tempted in your most recent experiences and see if there is a pattern in which temptation you are most provoked by.

- Is it something to satisfy a physical or unhealthy emotional need?
- Is it something you want to own or possess?
- Is it something that creates pride within you or exposes pride in your heart?

Column 3: My Reaction

Once you've listed an incident on your character inventory, list how you reacted to the incident. Did you get angry and act on it? Did you say things that may not have been the best choice of words? This column is where your character defects begin to appear. For example, if we tend to react in anger, maybe anger is something you may need to ask God to remove.

> And do not be conformed to this world, but be transformed by the renewing of your mind, so that you may prove what the will of God is, that which is good and acceptable and perfect. For through the grace given to me I say to everyone among you not to think more highly of himself than he ought to think; but to think so as to have sound judgement, as God has allotted to each a measure of faith. (Romans 12:2–3 NASB)

Column 4: Possible Response

So how do we stop reacting? What are we supposed to replace it with? The answer lies in the fruit of the Spirit: the Holy Spirit. In the previous lesson, we learned what these fruits are from Galatians 5:22–23. Now we get to see how to apply them.

After looking at each incident you have listed and your reaction to it, review the list of the fruits of the Spirit to see which ones, if any, you believe would have been a better way to respond to the situation you inventoried.

**Facilitator note: It is helpful to ask for a volunteer or volunteer one of your own instances to demonstrate how this assessment works.

Question: Pick an incident on your character inventory and a fruit you could have chosen to use in the moment. How do you think the moment would have been different?

We cannot control what happens in our lives or what others do. We cannot even control how we are tempted. We can't always control how we feel about something we experience. But we can control how we handle it: react or respond. That is the question to ask yourself. Although everything inside you may want to react negatively in the moment, seeing how this works, you see that you get to control your response and choose how you handle it. And that is empowering! It's *your* choice!

STEP 7

LESSON 12: PRAY TO TAKE AWAY

Stand firm therefore, having belted your waist with truth,
and having put on the breastplate of righteousness.
—Ephesians 6:14 (NASB)

Step 7: We humbly asked Him to remove our shortcomings.

At this point, you may have identified some shortcomings in your life.
Shortcomings are habits and/or character defects that have in the past
caused harm to you or others. This harm may have been physically,
mentally, emotionally, spiritually, and financially damaging.

We are not perfect beings. This step is not about becoming perfect.
It is, however, about becoming a better, healthier version of yourself.
When you hold on to those character defects for whatever reason,
you allow pain and chaos to remain in your life. It then breeds
negative thoughts about yourself and/or others, often leading right
back to guilt and shame down the road. The Bible tells us,

> And do not be conformed to this world, but be
> transformed by the renewing of your mind, so that you
> may prove what the will of God is, that which is good
> and acceptable and perfect. (Romans 12:2 NASB)

To "not be conformed to this world" is to not fall into the traps that may lead back to what you just came out of: addiction, trauma wounds, toxic relationships, and even the opinions or labels of others.

It is important to be transformed, in this case, by renewing your mind. Renewing your mind by allowing your character to be molded and changed is personal growth. You become more attentive to maintaining your personal peace rather than people-pleasing or worrying about what others may say or think of you. You may notice the fear of missing out beginning to have less of a hold on your choices.

When you seek God's will for your life start leaning into it, you prove His plans for you are "good and acceptable and perfect." You may not always understand them, but this is how faith grows: by trusting that God will help you along your journey if you invite Him along.

Asking God to remove your shortcomings doesn't just put the responsibility on God. When you ask God to remove these things, you may greatly benefit by putting in the work to keep these things from coming back into your life. A good place to begin is to look for solutions rather than chaos whenever situations arise.

Some reasons character defects or shortcomings return include the following:

- returning to people, places, things, or similar situations that have triggered these shortcomings in the past
- compromised boundaries
- toxic relationships
- suppressed anger
- unhealed trauma

Question: What shortcomings are you ready to change and ask God to remove from your life?

Question: Do you have any reservations about asking God to remove these things? If so, what are they?

This step is a moment of growth, and growth may be uncomfortable or even painful at times.

> For the moment, all discipline seems not to be pleasant, but painful; yet to those who have been trained by it, afterward it yields the peaceful fruit of righteousness. (Hebrews 12:11 NASB)

The goal is to remain in recovery and maintain peace in our lives. The Bible further tells us the following:

For a man's anger does not bring about the righteousness of God. (James 1:20 NASB)

> And the fruit of righteousness is sown in peace by those who make peace. (James 3:18 NASB)

Question: What are some ways to keep your shortcomings from returning in your life?

One who walks with integrity, practices righteousness, and speaks truth in his heart. He does not slander with his tongue, Nor do evil to his neighbor, Nor bring shame on his friend. (Psalm 15:2–3 NASB)

STEP 8

Lesson 13: Happiness, Joy, and Peace

And having strapped on your feet the
preparation of the gospel of peace.
—Ephesians 6:15 (NASB)

Step 8: We made a list of all persons we had harmed and became willing to make amends to them all.

If you recall, steps 4 and 5 began the process of putting on one peace boot and lacing it up. Now it's time to put on the other boot. Boots in the armor of God represent marching through life in peace. Doing a moral inventory and sharing it with someone is the beginning of healing. To continue on this journey, you now get to identify and become willing to make any necessary amends with God, yourself, and others to find peace.

Before diving into the identification process, let's look at the difference in happiness, joy, and peace.

Happiness is an emotion you may feel based on something that is going on around you. It is temporary, based on how long the event or circumstance around you lasts and continues to make you happy by its existence.

Joy is one of fruits of the Holy Spirit. It is an internal feeling of happiness and contentment despite what may be going on around you. Joy comes from walking with God and abiding in His love and His word.

> These things I have spoken to you so that my joy
> may be in you, and that your joy may be made full.
> (John 15:11 NASB)

You may have heard the saying "You can't pour from an empty cup." God made us to be full of joy, and joy comes from Him. If you feel your joy tank is running on empty or feeling more anxious or depressed, tell God. He wants to restore your joy, and it begins with spending time with Him, telling Him how you feel. Could the beginning of your amends process possibly be in making amends with God? If you need to seek forgiveness for anything past or present from Him, let me assure you that He so eagerly wants to hear from you! He wants nothing more than to fill you back up and restore your joy!

Question: Is it difficult to go to God with things you know you need to ask His forgiveness for? Why or why not?

Question: If you are holding a grudge against God at this point, why is it hard to let go of it?

> Then I will compensate you for the years That the
> swarming locust has eaten, The creeping locust, the
> stripping locust and the gnawing locust, My great
> army which I sent among you. (Joel 2:25 NASB)

How many years you allow the locusts to eat at your life depends on you. Will you humble your heart and make your amends with God first? Or will you keep holding on to it, allowing it to eat at the core of your joy?

Peace is also a fruit of the Holy Spirit. Peace means to be free of disturbance; a state or period in which there is no war or a war has ended. To be free of disturbances does not mean that you are problem free. It means that the external problems you face do not have to eat at your core. This war may be one that you feel toward God, others, or even yourself.

Sometimes the biggest war you will ever fight will be the one in your own mind: war with shame, guilt, confusion, frustration, areas of unforgiveness, worries, and fears. If you notice, none of these are what God wants for you. As long as you hold on to them or allow them to go unaddressed, they will continue to keep this war going on in your heart and mind, delaying true peace within.

Question: Describe a time when you felt peace in your life. If you have never honestly felt peace, what stands in your way of seeking it?

Question: Why is it hard to calm the war of thoughts that goes on in your mind?

It is very important to understand how your Heavenly Father sees you, allowing it to sink down into your heart.

But as many as received Him, to them He gave the right to become children of God, even to those who believe in His name. (John 1:12 NASB)

And I will be a father to you, And you shall be sons and daughters to Me," Says the Lord Almighty. (2 Corinthians 6:18 NASB)

These things I have spoken to you, so that in Me you may have peace. In the world you have tribulation, but take courage; I have overcome the world. (John 16:33 NASB)

No matter what tribulations you may experience in life, there are none too big for God to handle.

STEP 8

LESSON 14: IDENTIFY WHO AND WHAT

> And having strapped on your feet the
> preparation of the gospel of peace.
> —Ephesians 6:15 (NASB)

Step 8: We made a list of all persons we had harmed and became willing to make amends to them all.

It's time to identify all of the people you have harmed *and* become willing to make amends with them. Notice that this is a two-part step. Let's begin with part one: identify the people.

This requires being very honest with yourself. It helps to ask God to show you anything you may be in denial about, anything you may have forgotten, or anything you may be still unwilling to apologize for.

> Search me, O God, and know my heart; Put me to
> the test and know my anxious thoughts; And see if
> there is any hurtful way in me, And lead me in the
> everlasting way. (Psalm 139:23–24 NASB)

You may have hurt people who have hurt you. These people should be listed in your step 4 moral inventory. Go back over that inventory to identify who you may owe amends. Next, identify people you have harmed who may not have harmed you and may not be listed on your step 4 inventory. This harm could be physical, mental, emotional, spiritual, financial, etc. List these people in the chart below.

Who have I harmed?	What action did I take to cause them harm?

It is difficult to want to make amends with people when you may not be quite ready to let go of the anger or hurt you feel toward them. That is where the second part of this step becomes important: *becoming willing to make amends with them all.*

Question: What must happen for you to become willing to make amends with someone?

If you find yourself waiting for an apology from someone before you will apologize to them for your part, you may still have some forgiveness to do first. Some people try to forgive. They may even want to forgive, but they just can't seem to figure out how when the roots of the wound run so deep.

Forgiveness is giving someone grace. It doesn't mean they earned it or even deserve it. It doesn't mean they made something right with you first. It means you grant them grace over causing you that wound so that *you* can be free from the imprisonment of it. Holding on to the resentment is only affecting you. You are not getting back at them by refusing to forgive them.

Question: If unforgiveness has been your weapon to get back at them, is it working? What are you gaining from it in the meantime?

> And whenever you stand praying, forgive, if you have anything against anyone, so that your Father who is in heaven will also forgive you your offenses. (Mark 11:25 NASB)

For others, forgiving someone may cause you to feel vulnerable to be hurt in that same way again. Choosing to forgive someone does not mean they are free to do it again. It means you are forgiving the past action, but you must establish healthy boundaries for yourself so that you are not exposed to the potential hurt again while healing those wounds.

Question: Do you fear forgiving someone will cause you to feel vulnerable for the hurt to happen again? Give an example.

If we want to receive forgiveness, we must give forgiveness; however, that is often easier said than done. Let's go back to what we know. We know that hurt people tend to hurt other people in much the same way they have been hurt. Take a moment to examine the names of the people you have a hard time forgiving. What do you know about them? Do you know enough about their lives to know where they were hurt in their past? Do you think they acted on their hurt and in turn hurt you?

Know that this *does not* give anyone a free pass or an excuse to hurt you or anyone else. It does, however, explain many times *why* someone hurt you. If you have ever hurt someone innocently because you were acting on old hurt or anger that wasn't even caused by that person, you can surely relate.

In other situations, people often get angry when someone violates their value system, mainly their top five values.

***Facilitator note: Hand out the list of values in this lesson. Have participants identify their top five values. (This may take time for some participants. Others will finish quickly.) Ask for a volunteer to share their top five values. Once shared, ask him or her to recall a situation where he or she still feels angry because their values were violated. Ask them to rate their anger level on a scale of 1–5, with 5 being the highest level of anger they feel toward that person. Now ask him or her how many of their top values were violated by the person in that incident. Oftentimes, the numbers relate. For example, if three of their values were violated, anger may be at a level of 3.

Our values do not always align with other people's value systems. Furthermore, values do not always equal goodness. Some people value things that tear others down, promote self, and are damaging to themselves and others. Values get morphed by life experiences and how those experiences are processed. When our values do not align with others' values or vice versa, conflict may arise. It is important to learn the art of agreeing to disagree, knowing that their value systems came from some experiences you may or may not know anything about.

Question: Have you ever violated your own values? Give an example.

Just like learning to give others grace, we also must learn to show grace to ourselves when we have violated our own values. The point is not to beat ourselves up for it over and over but to really examine why it happened and what brought you to that moment so that you can be aware the next time the same or similar instance occurs. Holding unforgiveness to yourself holds on to self-shame until you finally extend forgiveness to *you*. If God can forgive it, why should you hold on to it?

For all have sinned and fall short of the glory of God. (Romans 3:23 NASB)

> The LORD is gracious and compassionate; Slow to anger and great in lovingkindness. (Psalm 145:8 NASB)

Question: Do you find it hard to forgive yourself? Why or why not?

As you finalize your amends list, pray for the willingness to make amends to them all in God's timing. We will discuss how to make amends in the next step.

> You have heard that it was said "YOU SHALL LOVE YOUR NEIGHBOR and hate your enemy." But I say to you, love your enemies and pray for those

who persecute you, so that you may prove yourselves to be sons of your Father who is in heaven; for He causes His sun to rise on the evil and the good, and sends rain on the righteous and the unrighteous. For if you love those who love you, what reward do you have? Even the tax collectors, do they not do the same? And if you greet only your brothers and sisters, what more are you doing than others? Even the Gentiles, do they not do the same? (Matthew 5:43–46 NASB)

Growth in recovery, in your walk with God, and in your life hinges on forgiveness: giving forgiveness and seeking forgiveness.

LIST OF VALUES

family	freedom	honesty/truth	courage
adventure	balance	security	kindness
loyalty	teamwork	fitness	professionalism
communication	relationships	creativity	learning
humanity	patience	success	change
respect	quality	prosperity/wealth	wellness
diversity	being heard	financial stability	spiritualism
gratitude	integrity	strength	grace
endurance	love	openness	effectiveness
religion	power	fun	order
affection	fame	advancement	cooperation
justice	humility	love of career	appreciation
joy	willingness	forgiveness	encouragement
intuition	work ethic	excitement	clarity
self-respect	compassion	peace	self-control
involvement	faith	leadership	wisdom
beauty	self-care	comfortable home	entrepreneurial
caring	be true	purposefulness	support
contentment	harmony	friendships	legacy
competition	sincerity	fairness	decisiveness
personal development			

STEP 9

LESSON 15: MENDING FENCES

> And having strapped on your feet the
> preparation of the gospel of peace.
> —Ephesians 6:15 (NASB)

Step 9: We made direct amends to such people whenever possible, except when to do so would injure them or others.

In steps 4 and 5, you put on one of your peace boots and laced it up. Now in steps 8 and 9, you are lacing up the other boot by becoming willing to make amends to those you have hurt. Forgiveness brings about peace.

At this point, you may have recognized those you are having a hard time forgiving while doing character inventory and the values exercise. If you have not been able to get to a place in your heart and mind where you are truly ready to forgive others, now is a good time to pray and ask God to help you with finding forgiveness for them. The Bible says,

> And whenever you stand praying, forgive, if you
> have anything against anyone, so that your Father
> who is in heaven will also forgive you for your
> offenses. (Mark 11:25 NASB)

We need to give forgiveness to receive forgiveness because that's what God did for us.

Step 9 is about making amends. This does not, however, guarantee people will forgive you just because you apologized for your wrongs. You must keep in mind that they are hurt, too, and could still be upset. People do not always heal at the same pace or forgive easily. It does, however, free you of the offense when you apologize for your part in it. Whether they forgive you or not becomes a matter of their healing between them and God.

It is very important to not have any expectations when making amends. If you approach someone expecting to receive an apology back, you can cause further resentment when your expectation is not met. This step *must* be focused on *your* part of the amends only, not theirs.

> If possible, so far as it depends on you, be at peace
> with all people. (Romans 12:18 NASB)

Prayerfully ask God to prepare the heart of the person with you whom you are making amends. And making amends is not something that needs to be rushed. You will know when the time is right for you to approach each person.

Question: What concerns do you have in making amends with others?

Some people you needed to make amends with may have passed away. In these situations, you may find healing by writing each one a letter to say what you wish you could say. You may even visit the gravesite when possible to read the letter there for closure. Or you may read it to your sponsor, coach, or accountability partner.

There also may be some people you do not need to make amends with face-to-face. If contacting someone from your past would cause harm to them or others in their lives now, you are not advised to do so. If reaching out to someone in your past who has caused you danger or harm and could do so again, you are not advised to make face-to-face amends. In both of these situations, writing them letters and reading these letters to your sponsor or coach provides relief and some closure. Your sponsor or coach should help you determine whether it may or may not be safe to send the letters once you have shared them.

Without some type of outlet to make your amends heard in some way, you may still hold these things inside. Doing so will potentially keep the negative self-talk going in your mind, hindering full peace in your life. It is important to take this step seriously. Writing letters is important just to let it leave you internally. You get to decide what you want to do with these letters.

> Do not fear, for I am with you; Do not be afraid, for I am your God. I will strengthen you, I will also help you, I will uphold you with My righteous right hand. (Isaiah 41:10 NASB)

Questions: Describe a time you made amends that did not end well.

Question: Have you ever made amends that ended well? What do you feel made it go well?

STEP 10

LESSON 16: RESTOCKING JOY

Stand firm therefore, having belted your waist with truth,
and having put on the breastplate of righteousness.
—Ephesians 6:14 (NASB)

Step 10: We continued to take personal inventory, and when we were
wrong, we promptly admitted it.

You may have found joy, peace, and/or relief from the amends you
made in step 9. Now the question becomes this: how do you keep
that joy flowing? Daily cleaning out any hurts, anger, resentments,
etc. that may have surfaced throughout the day helps keep your heart
and mind free so that you have room for peace in your life.

Peace I leave you; My peace I give you; not as the
world gives, do I give it to you. Do not let your
hearts be troubled, nor fearful. (John 14:27 NASB)

Daily inventory may be done in different ways, one of which is
journaling. Just scanning through the course of your day mentally
may leave the "little things" unaccounted for, causing a buildup of
resentments and hurts to go undetected. It's those little things that
easily build up into bigger issues down the road.

When we only process what happened in our day without acknowledging how it honestly made us feel, we risk leaving a critical part of the inventory undone. Journaling should cover the event, how you felt about the event, and what action you need to take to keep your heart and mind clear. Maybe it's finding empathy toward the person who made you angry earlier in the day. Maybe you need to apologize for something or forgive someone for their actions. The longer you hold on to either situation, the more toxicity it breeds inside your heart and mind. Before long, you may find yourself hurting others because you have built-up hurt that remains.

While journaling, allow your thoughts to flow by thinking the thought and emotion through to the end until you find what is really bothering you about it. An easy way to get your thoughts going is to recall the events of your day, and when something you recall makes you feel some type of way, note it in your journal. Examples of journaling may be the following:

- Were you triggered by something that happened?
- Were there any situations that created a moment of fear or doubt and you reacted in ways that hurt someone around you?
- Does the hurt you feel actually hurt your heart or your pride?

Some people don't enjoy journaling or don't feel they have time to journal. Journaling does not look the same for everyone. If you are one of these people, it may be quick bullet points jotted down about your day that you feel you need to take care of by giving forgiveness or making amends. It may be an acknowledgment of situations you need to pray over for clarity on how to approach them. It is important to work this step in a way that works for you personally in an effort to keep this step as part of your day-to-day life.

Question: Have you ever written in a daily journal? Why or why not?

Question: What are some ways you plan to do daily inventory?

If you choose journaling, periodically review them for similar entries that occur frequently. For example, if you find that you are becoming angry over numerous things, could it be that you are dealing with something that has you resorting to anger throughout your days? Looking for patterns helps you see where you've been, where you are, and where you may be going. Reflecting can help you move forward.

***Facilitator note: Take this opportunity to brainstorm with the group to create a list of ideas participants have either found to work this step or ways they want to practice working this step. It is a good exercise for those who may be struggling privately with making personal daily inventory a practice.

Challenge: Try a form of daily inventory for twenty-one days that works for you, and review with your coach or sponsor. Discuss what worked and what didn't work so well. If this step was a struggle, brainstorm options that may work best for you with your coach or sponsor. This step takes dedication. The more dedicated you are to it, the more at peace you may feel, and dedication will come from how meaningful it becomes to you!

> Do not let kindness and truth leave you; Bind them around your neck, Write them on the tablet of your heart. So you will find favor and a good reputation in the sight of God and man. Trust in the LORD with all your heart And do not lean on your own understanding. In all your ways acknowledge Him, And He will make your paths straight. (Proverbs 3:3–6 NASB)

STEP 11

LESSON 17: REPORTING IN

And take the helmet of salvation and the sword
of the Spirit, which is the word of God.
—Ephesians 6:17 (NASB)

Step 11: We sought, through prayer and meditation, to improve our conscientious contact with God, praying only for knowledge of His will for us and the power to carry that out.

The success of any army is largely dependent upon how well the army has prepared for battle. There are several key factors involved in preparation. These include training, communication, and planning.

Training

You have been in training to maintain your recovery from the moment you decided to enter recovery. Each step you have made up to this point has been training you to be a soldier for your own sobriety. You have put in the "boot camp" time. You have also gained stamina and endurance training to keep fighting for sobriety because maintaining sobriety isn't easy. Also, working a recovery program has hopefully freed up room in your heart and mind for God if you allow it. The Bible tells us,

I will instruct you and teach you in the way which you should go; I will advise you with My eye upon you. (Psalm 32:8 NASB)

Question: What have you learned since you have been in recovery to help you continue fighting for your sobriety?

Communication

Communication with God is important to maintaining recovery. Asking God to guide you may be the very thing that saves your life when you find yourself in territory that isn't comfortable, something feels too familiar, or you feel fear, confusion, or worry. But it does not do any good to ask if you aren't prepared to listen. Sometimes we already know the answer, but we don't want to hear it because there is a part of us that still wants to do what we know we don't need to do. And because of that, often we make God the last One we go to for instruction or guidance. This is not just a matter of right or wrong. It is a matter if life or death when it comes to recovery. It's a matter of safety or danger. God wants to keep us safe. He knows exactly what we need in any given situation, if we will just ask Him for help in those moments.

No temptation has overtaken you except something common to mankind; and God is faithful, so He will not allow you to be tempted beyond what you are able, but with the temptation will provide the way of escape also, so that you will be able to endure it. (1 Corinthians 10:13 NASB)

God will provide you a way out of temptation. We just need to ask Him and then look for it. It's up to us if we take the way out away from the temptation.

Question: Is it difficult for you to ask God for help? Why or why not?

Staying in contact with God is not just for the tough times of life. Thanking God for those things you are grateful for, praying for wisdom to know how to handle situations, praying for protection, and praying for others are also reasons you may remain in contact with God.

Planning

Just as soldiers receive orders from their commanders, we have been given a plan to guide our lives. This plan is the Bible. The more soldiers study the plan and remain in contact with their commander for instruction, the better prepared they are to face the enemy. Recovery and life are no different.

The Bible has direction for anything we face in this life today. The word of God truly is a road map for us to live by. Granted, the *what* of our situations may be different, but the emotions and internal struggles are the same and have remained the same all throughout time. The more you study the Bible, the more you learn what their struggles were, how they handled them, and what the outcomes were. You also see how Jesus said to handle each situation that comes our way. The real questions are these: Will you continue to be teachable? Will you choose to learn more, hear more, and stay close to your Commander to keep you safe and your paths straight? It will make you a more effective soldier for your recovery.

Question: Some people have trouble reading their Bible for different reasons. Maybe it's time. Maybe it is difficulty understanding it. Maybe you don't enjoy reading. Is it difficult for you to want to read your Bible? Why or why not?

Whether you choose to pray, meditate, read your Bible and/or devotionals, listen to motivational messages, or draw close to God in nature, it is important to remain in contact with God to keep your heart and mind in healthy places. It is too easy to become burned out with recovery when we leave this step out.

Question: What are some ways you remain in contact with God?

STEP 12

LESSON 18: SUITED FOR BATTLE

In addition to all, taking up the shield of faith with which you will be able to extinguish all the flaming arrows of the evil one.
—Ephesians 6:16 (NASB)

Step 12: Having had a spiritual awakening as the results of these steps, we try to carry this message to others and to practice these principles in all our affairs.

It is quite exciting when you've reached step 12 of any twelve-step program. The moment often comes with feelings of excitement, accomplishment, relief, and freedom. Some may even feel a since of nervousness, asking themselves, "Can I keep this up?" or "Where do I go from here?" Just as the step indicates, recovery is a way of life going forward.

This step is more than the victory moment or a destination you just achieved. There are actually two parts to this step: carrying this message to others and practicing what you've learned in all of your affairs. It's time to decide what that means for you personally.

Helping Others

You are now at the final step of this program. For some of you, you may have previously completed other twelve-step programs and this time around has been for maintenance in maintaining your recovery. Either way, you are now able to sponsor others entering a twelve-step program. You may help others by being an accountability partner. You may also become involved in other areas of service for recovery or even make a career out of it.

As this step indicates, by now you should have had some type of spiritual awakening if you have worked these steps fully. Being a spiritual support for others is another important way of helping others. A spiritual supporter may provide prayers, words of encouragement, motivation, or just being a listening ear for someone struggling. It may also include being willing to share your experience of how God brought you through tough moments.

You may share your story at meetings, one on one, by writing a book, or by speaking at events to name a few. Talk with your sponsor if/ when you become ready to share your story. They should provide guidance for you.

Remaining active in recovery is the *best* way to safeguard against relapse. Just recall how important it was for you when you first began your recovery to be surrounded by others who were once where you were. You may serve as this same support for others and hopefully enjoy doing so!

Question: Is it difficult for you to support others? Why or why not?

Question: What are some ways you would like to help others?

As you begin to support or sponsor others, do not neglect your own self-care. If you are not in a good place, you can't help others who need it. Also, remember to set healthy boundaries so that you do not find yourself compromising your own recovery. Discuss both of these with your sponsor or coach frequently for accountability. They should be able to bring awareness to any potential issues that may go undetected.

Continue Practicing

Some people become burned out at this point. They want a break or want to see if they can manage on their own. I encourage you to talk to your sponsor or coach if you feel this way, to discuss the pros and cons for you personally of continuing a program or taking a break.

Many in recovery have said that when we think we don't need a program, that is when we need it the most. But when we try it on our own for a while, we tend to begin slipping into old patterns and habits and eventually compromise when we don't have that layer of accountability.

It is important to stay in contact with your sponsor for "check-in" moments. They are there to help you stay accountable.

Question: What are some ways you continue practicing these principles in your day-to-day life?

Question: What advice would you give someone experiencing burnout?

Allowing God in all of your affairs gives Him the platform to grow your faith shield as you journey through life. When you recall how you prayed, how He answered, and how He has your best interests at heart, even when it may not be what you want, your faith becomes stronger each time. If you don't allow Him in your life, the faith you have gained through your recovery may weaken, causing you to rely on yourself or others again. You risk feeling alone or isolated at times.

Continue to do what works for you to keep you sober minded, so that you stay sober physically and mentally.

Congratulations! You have completed the twelve steps of armor and are ready to be a soldier fighting for your recovery and helping others fight for theirs!

> Go therefore and make disciples of all the nations … teaching them to follow all that I commanded you; and behold, I am with you always, even to the end of the age. (Matthew 28:19–20 NASB)

Printed in the United States
by Baker & Taylor Publisher Services